The Highway of Life

A 30-Day Devotional for the Driven Man

By Josmar Pereira

The Highway of Life: A 30-Day Devotional for the Driven Man

Printed in the United States of America. First Edition: March 2026

Dedication

This book is dedicated to my wife, Janete, who has been my constant passenger and partner on every mile of this journey. Your strength and your stride have kept me moving forward.

To my daughters, grandkids, and the future generations of our family: May you always keep your eyes on the Map and never lose sight of the Eternal City.

And to the Men of the Road: To those who have hit the wall, those who are redlining their engines, and those who are simply lost in the fog. May this roadmap help you pull over, find the Master Mechanic, and get back on the only way home.

Table of Contents

Introduction

The Roadmap to Your Soul

The Choice to Pull Over

If you are holding this book in your hands, congratulations. You've taken the single most crucial step a driver can: deciding to stop your vehicle. In a world that demands we keep the pedal to the floor, choosing to stop and check your alignment is the first step toward a life that lasts.

The Highway and the Vehicle

This book is about the road we all travel, the high speed, often chaotic journey of life. We can compare our existence to a vast highway, and ourselves to the vehicles navigating it. From the moment we are "born" onto the pavement, we are in a constant state of motion, trying to reach a destination we often haven't even defined.

The Problem: Redlining in the Dark

The problem many of us face is that we are driving blindly. We hit the road at full speed, ignoring the flickering "Check Engine" lights of our marriages, our health, and our peace of mind. We treat our families like cargo, our careers like a racetrack, and our pride like high-octane fuel. But eventually, every man who drives by his own rules hits a wall. Whether it's a career crash, a broken home, or a spiritual burnout, the "Collision" is inevitable when we ignore the Map.

A Glimpse of the Journey

In the pages ahead, we will explore the "Assembly Line" of our youth, the dangerous "Road Rage" of blind ambition, and the "Shortcuts" that lead us deep into the woods of destruction. You will learn to identify the warning signs on your own dashboard and, most importantly, how to surrender the keys to the Master Mechanic before the wreckage becomes permanent.

From the Driver's Seat: My Perspective

I don't write these words as a distant lecturer, but as a fellow traveler who has spent decades behind the wheel. As a veteran of the United States Army, I understand what it means to follow a mission under pressure. As a business owner and a family man, I have felt the vibration in the steering wheel when my priorities were out of alignment. I have seen the "Collision" firsthand, and I have had to stand on the shoulder of the road and admit I was lost. My expertise wasn't gained in a classroom; it was forged through miles of trial, error, and eventual restoration by the Grace of God.

The Benefit: A New Alignment

The information in this devotional is designed to do more than just provide a good story. It is a toolkit for your soul. By applying these reflections, you will gain a clearer vision of your true destination. You will learn how to protect your "passengers", the people who matter the most and how to tune your ears to a GPS that never fails, even in the thickest fog.

Proven Results

This roadmap has transformed my own life, taking me from a man driving on ego to a man driving by the Map. I have shared these "Road Reflections" with men who were on the verge of total engine failure, men whose marriages were stalled and whose spirits were broken. I have watched them pull into the "Body Shop" of faith and emerge with a renewed purpose and a steady hand on the wheel. They didn't just get their lives back; they got a new engine.

Start the Engine

The road is waiting, but this time, you aren't driving alone. Turn the page, open the Map, and let's begin the journey toward the Eternal City. It's time to drive.

Talk to the Driver

Before You Pray

I want to tell you something before your first prayer in this book. I want to tell you what I wish someone had told me before. I spent years believing that God was silent, distant, and dangerous to approach.

I grew up Catholic in Brazil. The church I knew was built on silence and ritual. You did not open your mouth inside those walls, unless you were told to repeat specific religious ritualistic prayers. You did not speak to God directly, you went through the priest, through the saint, through the statue. Prayer was something you did in secret, in whispers, with a rosary in your hands and your eyes on the floor. And the Bible, that book was not for ordinary people. My own mother warned us that reading it could make a person go crazy. It was to be handled with care, treated with fear, kept at a distance. The God I was taught about was not a Father you could talk to. He was a Judge you tried not to anger.

The confessional was where you whispered your sins to a man behind a curtain, and absolution came from the man with a penance of Hail Mary's or other repetitiously prayer, it was never from God. There was no freedom in it. There was management. Religion without relationship. Ritual without rescue. And when the church was done with you, the world picked up where it left off, adding stone after stone to the burden bag until the weight of it became unbearable.

I know what that weight feels like. I know it because on November 25, 2005, I was sitting in my car in my own driveway in Lynn, Massachusetts, with a demon whispering in my ear that my family would be better off without me. The castle I had built on sand was collapsing. The business, the house, the marriage, all of it crumbling. And the voice said: Go ahead. Do it. They won't miss you.

That was the bottom of my road.

But God, oh God, He had never left. Not once. Not through the Catholic silence, not through the spiritism and the Macumba and the mixed-up altar of Buddha and saints in my father's house, not through the years of hollow Sunday mass attendance, not through the driveway. While I was listening to the enemy's voice, my wife Janete was on her knees in our living room with our daughters, praying to a God she was just beginning to know. She had gone to the Catholic church for help and been sent to a statue. She walked out of that empty religion and went home — and there, on her knees in our living room, she talked directly to the living God for the first time. And God answered her.

What happened next the hospital, the Bible lying on a table that my thirsty spirit could not resist, the Sunday after Thanksgiving when I found myself on my knees with my clothes soaked like I had been thrown into deep water — that was not religion. That was rescue.

And in that moment, I learned something that changed everything: God was not silent. He had been listening the whole time. I just had never been taught that I could speak.

> *"Therefore if the Son makes you free, you shall be free indeed." — John 8:36 (NKJV)*

The pain washed away. The guilt is gone. The burden bag dropped at the foot of the cross and never picked up again.

So before you pray the prayers in this book, I want you to hear this from a man who grew up believing God was too holy to talk to directly: He is not. He is your Father. He is leaning in right now. He is not waiting for you to get the words right or the posture correct or the religious formula memorized. He is waiting for you to open your mouth and say what is actually true.

Talk to Him out loud. Not in a whisper. Not in secret. Not through a priest or a saint or a formula. Just you and your Father, on the side of the road, honest about where you are and what you need.

He is listening. He has always been listening.

God Cares for You

> *"Casting all your care upon Him, for He cares for you." 1 Peter 5:7 (NKJV)*

"Look at the birds of the air, for they neither sow nor reap nor gather into barns; yet your heavenly Father feeds them. Are you not of more value than they?" Matthew 6:26 (NKJV)
"Even to your old age, I am He, and even to gray hairs I will carry you. I have made, and I will bear; even I will carry and will deliver you." Isaiah 46:4 (NKJV)

God Listens

"Now this is the confidence that we have in Him, that if we ask anything according to His will, He hears us. And if we know that He hears us, whatever we ask, we know that we have the petitions that we have asked of Him." 1 John 5:14-15 (NKJV)

"I love the Lord, because He has heard my voice and my supplications. Because He has inclined His ear to me, therefore I will call upon Him as long as
I live." Psalm 116:1-2 (NKJV)

"Then you will call upon Me and go and pray to Me, and I will listen to you." Jeremiah 29:12 (NKJV)

God Invites You to Speak

"Be anxious for nothing, but in everything by prayer and supplication, with thanksgiving, let your requests be made known to God; and the peace of God, which surpasses all understanding, will guard your hearts and your minds through Christ Jesus." Philippians 4:6-7 (NKJV)

"In this manner, therefore, pray: Our Father in heaven, hallowed be Your name. Your kingdom come. Your will be done on earth as it is in heaven. Give us this day our daily bread. And forgive us our debts, as we forgive our debtors. And do not lead us into temptation, but deliver us from the evil one. For Yours is the kingdom and the power and the glory forever. Amen." Matthew 6:9-13 (NKJV)

"Pray without ceasing." 1 Thessalonians 5:17 (NKJV)

Now open your mouth. Talk to your Father in Heaven. He is already in the car with you.

Chapter 1

The Assembly Line

(The Myth of Invincibility)

When we are young, we are like a car fresh off the assembly line. The engine is clean, the tires have full tread, and we believe our fuel tank is bottomless. We hit the road at full speed, disregarding the "speed limits" and the counsel of the elders who have driven these miles before us.

Our only goal is to enjoy the ride. We make our "Pit Stops" in the wrong places — the bars, the discos, the neon-lit stops that offer high-octane rush but low-quality sustenance. We think we are experts because we drive with confidence. We play the game safe, or we redline the engine, but we all share one delusion: we think we are the ones in control of the road.

The Map (Scripture):

> *"There is a way that seems right to a man, but its end is the way of death." Proverbs 14:12 (NKJV)*

A Fellow Traveler: Solomon, Son of David

King Solomon began his reign as the wisest man on earth, freshly anointed, full of promise, and given a divine mandate. Yet in Ecclesiastes, written near the end of his life, he looked back at the Assembly Line years with devastating honesty. He had tried wine, women, wealth, architecture, and achievement — every pit stop the young man believes will satisfy. "I denied myself nothing my eyes desired; I refused my heart no pleasure," he wrote. "Yet when I surveyed all that my hands had done and what I had toiled to achieve, everything was meaningless, a chasing after the wind." Solomon's life is the autobiography of the Assembly Line taken to its logical conclusion. The man with the fastest car and unlimited fuel still arrived at the same emptiness when he drove for himself instead of for God. His final word was simple: "Fear God and keep his commandments, for this is the duty of all mankind." The Assembly Line is not the destination. It is the starting point.

The Rearview Mirror (Reflections):

1. What "pit stops" did you make in your early years that you are still paying for today?

2. What counsel from an elder did you dismiss when you were young that turned out to be exactly right?

3. If you could speak to a young man standing at the Assembly Line right now, what is the one thing you would tell him before he hits the road?

Talk to the Driver (Prayer):

Lord, I have to be honest with You. When I was young, I thought I had it all figured out. I thought the fuel tank was bottomless and the road belonged to me. I made pit stops in all the wrong places, and I am still paying for some of those choices today. I am not asking You to erase the miles — I am asking You to redeem them. Take everything I have driven through and use it for something that matters. I do not want to just enjoy the ride anymore. I want to drive for a purpose that is bigger than me. Show me the right road. I am listening. Amen.

Chapter 2

Road Rage

(The High Cost of Ambition)

As "Kings of our own destiny," we drive as if the road belongs to us. We develop a spiritual "Road Rage." We decide there is no room for anyone to pass us or stay in front of us. This is how we deal with business, family, and relationships.

We ignore the "Stop" signs of our conscience and the "Yield" signs of our marriage. We plow ahead to fulfill our goals, putting the "Promotion" and the "Title" in the front seat while our wife and children are relegated to the back. We feel offended if someone else gets the recognition we wanted. This rage impairs our judgment, leading us to take drastic measures to stay "in the lead."

The Map (Scripture):

> *"For what will it profit a man if he gains the whole world, and loses his own soul?" — Mark 8:36 (NKJV)*

A Fellow Traveler: Howard Hughes

Howard Hughes was one of the most driven men of the 20th century — aviator, filmmaker, engineer, and billionaire. He broke air speed records, built a media empire, and accumulated more wealth than almost any man alive. He was the living definition of a man who believed the road belonged to him. But the Road Rage of his ambition eventually consumed everything. His obsessive need for control led to severe OCD, a total withdrawal from society, and a final decade spent in complete isolation, his empire crumbling around him while he lived in darkened hotel rooms, terrified of the world he had once dominated. He died in 1976 at 70 years old, severely malnourished, his body riddled with the effects of years of neglect. He had gained a world and lost everything that mattered. The "passengers" in his life — relationships, health, peace of mind, connection — had all been pushed off the road decades before. The destination he arrived at was not the one he had been racing toward.

The Rearview Mirror (Reflections):

1. Who have you "cut off" or pushed onto the shoulder of the road recently in your pursuit of success?
2. If your "Passengers" (family) could speak freely right now, would they say they feel safe with you behind the wheel?
3. What would you have to slow down to protect the people in your car?

Talk to the Driver (Prayer):

Father, I must admit that there are people I have pushed off the road in my pursuit of getting ahead. My family has felt it. The people closest to me have felt it. Forgive me for driving like the road belonged to me. Help me slow down. Help me make room. Help me become the kind of man whose family feels safe in the car, not left behind on the shoulder. Change the way I drive. Starting today. Amen.

Chapter 3

The Wrong Turn

(The Shortcut to Destruction)

Road rage and pride eventually lead to a "Wrong Turn." We see a path that looks like a shortcut, an ethical compromise, a secret habit, a "moment of weakness." We miscalculate. The road suddenly becomes darker and rougher.

The engine RPMs become so loud they muffle the warning signs. The dashboard lights up with "Check Engine" and "Low Oil" warnings, but we tell ourselves, "I can fix it." We neglect the Manual (The Word) and the directions of others. We think we are still on the main highway, but we are deep in the woods, heading for a dead end.

The Map (Scripture):

> *"The way of a guilty man is perverse; but as for the pure, his work is right." Proverbs 21:8 (NKJV)*

A Fellow Traveler: King Saul

King Saul was the first man chosen to drive the nation of Israel. He had the right vehicle and a clear route, but when the pressure mounted, he took a devastating shortcut. After a conquest, Saul became anxious because the prophet Samuel was delayed, Saul ignored the Manual. Instead of waiting for God's timing, he forced an ethical compromise and offered the sacrifice himself. He rationalized the wrong turn, telling himself, "I felt compelled to do it." It was the ultimate "I can fix it" moment. That first shortcut led to a pattern. He covered his disobedience with religious excuses. The dashboard lights were flashing red, and the warning bells of the prophets were ringing, but

Saul's need for control muffled the sound. He thought he was still on the main highway, but he was actually steering his kingdom deep into the dark woods of paranoia and isolation. He was accelerating straight toward a dead end, completely convinced he was still the one in control.

The Rearview Mirror (Reflections):

1. What "Dashboard Light" (guilt, anxiety, tension) have you been ignoring lately?
2. Is there a "Shortcut" you are currently taking that you are keeping secret from everyone else in the car?
3. What would it cost you to get back on the right road?

Talk to the Driver (Prayer):

Lord, I am standing in the wreckage right now and I do not want to be honest about how much of this is my fault. I told myself nobody would know. But You already know. I know my hands are no longer enough. I don't know what will happen next, but I know I need a rescue. Amen.

Chapter 4

The Collision

(The Reality of the Wreckage)

Then, we hit it. The "Collision" happens. We step out of the car and look around — it is a mess. The marriage is shaken, the career is at peril, the family is broken. We try to pick up the pieces, but they are scattered all over the pavement.

Our first instinct is to blame the "Other Driver." We say, "They took advantage of me! I am not responsible for this failed business or this broken home!" But (The Law) says otherwise. The Judge takes notice. The Accuser presents the record. When the "GPS Logs" are opened, they show exactly where we left the path. We realize we took the World's advice to "enjoy life to the fullest" at the expense of the Truth.

The Map (Scripture):

> *"For we must all appear before the judgment seat of Christ, that each one may receive the things done in the body, according to what he has done, whether good or bad." — 2 Corinthians 5:10 (NKJV)*

A Fellow Traveler: Samson

Samson was the strongest man who ever lived — a man set apart by God from birth for a specific mission, given supernatural power, and equipped for a destiny of deliverance. He drove like a man who believed his strength made him invincible. He ignored every warning sign. He made pit stops in enemy territory. He told his secrets to a woman whose loyalties he had every reason to question. The Collision, when it came, was total: betrayal, capture, blinded, chained, humiliated, grinding grain like an animal in a Philistine prison. The man who had destroyed a thousand enemies with the jawbone of a donkey was brought down by a whispered secret and a pair of scissors. Yet Samson's story does not end in the prison. It ends in the rubble of the temple of Dagon, where a blinded, humbled man called out to God one final time — and God answered. The Collision did not disqualify Samson. It became the context for his greatest act. The wreckage is not the end of the road.

The Rearview Mirror (Reflections):

1. In the "Wreckage" of your current situation, are you still trying to blame the other person, or are you ready to look at your own driving record?
2. What is the "Cost" to get your life fixed, and are you willing to admit you can't pay it yourself?
3. What would it look like to call out to God from wherever you are right now, even from the prison?

Talk to the Driver (Prayer):

Lord, I am standing in the wreckage right now and I do not want to be honest about how much of this is my fault. It is easier to point at the other driver. But when I open the GPS logs of my own choices, I know the truth. I left the path. I am not asking You to fix everything immediately. I am asking You to forgive me first. Take the record of my failures and nail it to the cross. And then help me pick up the pieces with You beside me. Amen.

Chapter 5

The Tow Truck

(The End of Self-Reliance)

After the collision, we stand on the shoulder of the road, looking at the smoke rising from the hood. Our first instinct is still to "fix it." We are "Kings of the Road" who have suddenly lost our kingdom.

The most difficult moment for a man is the moment he realizes his vehicle is a "Total Loss" under his own management. We have to call for a Tow Truck. To do this, we have to admit we are stranded. This is the moment of Humility. The Tow Truck doesn't care about your titles or your excuses. It only cares that you are hooked up to the Chain of Grace.

The Map (Scripture):

> *"God resists the proud, but gives grace to the humble." — James 4:6 (NKJV)*

A Fellow Traveler: Nebuchadnezzar

Nebuchadnezzar was the greatest king of the ancient world—the builder of the Hanging Gardens, the conqueror of nations, the man whose empire stretched from the Persian Gulf to the Mediterranean Sea. He stood on the roof of his palace, surveyed the city he had built, and said, "Is not this the great Babylon I have built as the royal residence, by my mighty power and for the glory of my majesty?".

In that exact moment, his engine failed completely. God struck him with madness. For seven years, the most powerful man on earth lived like an animal in the field, eating grass, his hair growing like eagle feathers, his nails like bird claws.

It looked like total destruction, but it was actually the Tow Truck arriving. God pulled him off the road to save him from his own pride. At the end of the seven years, Nebuchadnezzar looked up and acknowledged the God of heaven. His sanity was restored, his kingdom was returned, and he issued a decree praising the King of heaven across his entire empire. The man who had been brought the lowest became the one who proclaimed the highest. The Tow Truck does not destroy your kingdom. It rescues it from the driver who was wrecking it.

The Rearview Mirror (Reflections):

1. Why is it so hard for you to admit that your "engine" has failed?
2. Humility isn't thinking less of your "car"; it's thinking of your "car" less and focusing on the One who is rescuing you. What would that shift look like in your daily life?
3. What would you have to release in order to be hooked up to the Chain of Grace right now?

Talk to the Driver (Prayer):

God, this is hard for me to say out loud. I have spent my entire life being the man who handles things. And right now I am standing on the side of the road with a vehicle that is a total loss, and I have nothing left. I cannot fix this one. I am asking You to send the Tow Truck. I am hooking myself up to Your grace right now, and I am letting go of the wheel. I do not know where You are taking me. But I know I cannot stay here. Come and get me. Amen.

Chapter 6

The Body Shop

(The Pain of Restoration)

Once the car is at the shop, the real work begins. The Master Mechanic doesn't just paint over the scratches; He tears the car down to the frame. He looks at the "Bent Axle" of your character and the "Cracked Block" of your heart.

This part of the journey is slow. It feels like you aren't moving at all. You see other cars "cruising along" outside the shop window, and you feel left behind. But the Mechanic knows that if He sends you back out with a broken frame, you'll just crash again at the next curve. This is the season of Sanctification.

The Map (Scripture):

> *"being confident of this very thing, that He who has begun a good work in you will complete it until the day of Jesus Christ." — Philippians 1:6 (NKJV)*

A Fellow Traveler: John Newton

John Newton spent years in the slave trade before his conversion, and even after coming to faith, he did not immediately leave the trade a fact he later described with deep shame. The Body Shop was not instant for Newton. God worked slowly, methodically, tearing him down to the frame over years of gradual conviction. Newton spent 34 years as a minister before he finally found the courage to testify publicly before Parliament about the horrors of the trade, he had participated in. The Mechanic was not done with him until he was 82 years old, nearly blind, and still preaching. When asked why he continued despite his failing health, Newton replied: "My memory is nearly gone, but I remember two things: that I am a great sinner, and that Christ is a great Saviour."[1] That is a man who spent his entire life in the Body Shop, being rebuilt from the frame up. The work was slow. It was thorough. And it produced a vehicle whose song "Amazing Grace" has carried more people toward the Eternal City than perhaps any other words ever written.

The Rearview Mirror (Reflections):

1. What part of your "inner engine" is God currently working on?
2. Are you trying to rush the Mechanic? Why are you in such a hurry to get back on the road before the repairs are finished?
3. What would it look like to fully cooperate with the work God is doing in you right now, instead of resisting it?

Talk to the Driver (Prayer):

Father, being in the Body Shop is not comfortable. I want to be back on the road. But I know that if You send me back out before the work is done, I will just crash again. So I am asking You for the one thing I find hardest: patience. Do the work You need to do. Take as long as You need. Tear down whatever needs to come down. I trust the Mechanic more than I trust my own timeline.

Finish the work. I am not going anywhere. Amen.

---

[1] Steve Turner, *Amazing Grace: John Newton, Slavery, and the World's Most Enduring Song* (New York: HarperOne, 2002), 223.

Chapter 7

The New GPS

(The Voice Above the Noise)

As we hit the road again, the first thing we notice is the noise. The world is still loud. The "Radios" of culture are still screaming for us to go faster, buy more, and ignore the signs. But this time, we've installed a new GPS: God-Prescribed Steps.

In the past, we turned the volume of the world up so loud we couldn't hear the directions. **We navigated entirely by our own ego, shoving God out of the passenger seat.** Now, we learn to listen to the 'Still, Small Voice' of the Navigator.

When the GPS says "Yield," we yield. When it says "Recalculating," we listen. We no longer drive by sight; we drive by the Map.

The Map (Scripture):

> *"Your word is a lamp to my feet and a light to my path." — Psalm 119:105 (NKJV)*

A Fellow Traveler: George Muller

George Muller was a 19th century minister in Bristol, England, who became one of the most documented examples of a man who drove entirely by the GPS of God's Word and prayer. He established orphanages that housed over 10,000 children over his lifetime, never once making a public appeal for funds. Instead, he prayed specifically and privately, kept meticulous records of every answered prayer, and trusted the Navigator completely. On one occasion, with no food in the house and hundreds of hungry children at breakfast, Muller thanked God for the food before any had arrived. Minutes later, a baker knocked at the door with fresh bread, followed by a milkman whose cart had broken down outside and who offered his milk rather than let it spoil. Muller's journals recorded over 50,000 specific answers to prayer. He drove 70 years of ministry by the GPS alone and arrived at the age of 92 having never taken the wheel back. The Still, Small Voice, when followed consistently, never leads anywhere but forward.

The Rearview Mirror (Reflections):

1. When "World's Radio" starts playing a song that tells you to take a shortcut, how do you tune back into the GPS?
2. Have you checked your "Map" (The Bible) today?
3. What is one specific area where you need to turn the volume of the world down and listen to the Navigator's voice this week?

Talk to the Driver (Prayer):

Lord, the world is loud today, and I confess I have been turning the volume up instead of turning it out. Right now, I am turning it down. I want to hear Your voice above everything else. Recalibrate my GPS. When I start drifting, pull me back.
When I am tempted to take a shortcut, remind me of the destination. Be my Navigator today. I will follow where You lead. Amen.

Chapter 8

The Final Destination

(The Eternal City)

The road doesn't go on forever. Every highway has an end. As we drive now, we aren't driving for the "Promotion" or the "Title" anymore. We are driving for the Homecoming.

The Eternal City is the place where the road is finally smooth, the engine never fails, and the "Collisions" of this life are forgotten. We drive with our "Passengers" now our family and friends teaching them how to read the Map so we can all arrive together. We aren't "Kings of the Road" anymore; we are just travelers, grateful for the Grace that kept us from the "Path of Destruction" and guided us to "The Way."

The Map (Scripture):

> *"For our citizenship is in heaven, from which we also eagerly wait for the Savior, the Lord Jesus Christ." — Philippians 3:20 (NKJV)*

A Fellow Traveler: Stephen, the First Martyr

Stephen was a man full of faith and the Holy Spirit, chosen to serve the early church in Jerusalem. When he was arrested and brought before the Sanhedrin, he preached the most comprehensive sermon in the book of Acts — a complete history of God's faithfulness on the road from Abraham to Christ — and then declared that he saw the Son of Man standing at the right hand of God. The crowd dragged him outside the city and stoned him to death. As the rocks fell, Stephen knelt and prayed, "Lord, do not hold this sin against them." And then he fell asleep. No man in Scripture more clearly demonstrates what it looks like to arrive at the Final Destination with the wheel still in the right hands. Stephen did not arrive in panic or regret. He arrived looking up

— eyes already on the Eternal City before his body hit the ground. Among the witnesses holding the coats of the men who threw the stones was a young man named Saul of Tarsus. That moment planted a seed that later became the Apostle Paul. Stephen's final mile touched every mile that followed.

The Rearview Mirror (Reflections):

1. If your journey ended today, would you be confident that you were on the road to the Eternal City?
2. Who is sitting in your passenger seat that needs to see you driving by faith?
3. What would it look like to live every day this week as if the Final Destination is real closer than you think, and worth every mile of the road?

Talk to the Driver (Prayer):

Father, help me lift my eyes today and remember the Eternal City. Help me drive in a way that my passengers the people I love can see where we are headed and want to go there too. I do not want to arrive alone. Keep my eyes on the destination. And let my driving today point everyone in my vehicle toward home. Amen.

Chapter 9

The Rest Stop

(Knowing When to Pause)

Every highway has a rest stop. It is not a sign of weakness to pull off; it is a sign of wisdom. The problem is that most driven men treat the rest stop like a failure. We were taught that the engine should always be running, that idle time is wasted time, and that the man who stops first loses the race.

But a vehicle that never rests will overheat. A driver who never sleeps will drift into the other lane. God designed rest into the fabric of creation itself — not as an afterthought, but as a cornerstone. The Sabbath was not a suggestion. It was a command built into the very rhythm of the universe. Yet we drive past it every week, telling ourselves we will rest when we arrive.

The tragedy is that many men never arrive. They die behind the wheel, still accelerating, still pushing, still proving. The rest stop is not the end of the journey. It is where you check your oil, stretch your legs, drink some water, and remember why you are driving in the first place. A rested driver is a focused driver. And a focused driver gets where he is going.

The Map (Scripture):

> *"Come to Me, all you who labor and are heavy laden, and I will give you rest." Matthew 11:28 (NKJV)*

A Fellow Traveler: A.W. Tozer

A.W. Tozer was one of the most prolific and respected Christian voices of the 20th century, yet he was known not for his busyness but for his stillness. At the height of his influence, when invitations flooded his desk and his books were selling across the world, Tozer maintained a discipline of daily solitude and prayer that alarmed his peers. He would often spend hours in silence before God before writing a single word. When asked how he produced such depth, he replied that he had simply learned to stop and listen[2]. Tozer understood that the voice of God was not found in the noise of ministry achievement it was found in the rest stop. He died in 1963, not exhausted and burned out, but full. His books still speak today because he refused to drive past the rest that God offered.

The Rearview Mirror (Reflections):

1. When was the last time you intentionally stopped — not because you were forced to, but because you chose to rest in God?

2. What are you afraid will happen if you slow down? What does that fear reveal about who you think is really in control of the road?

3. What would it look like to build one true "Rest Stop" into your week, every week, starting now?

Talk to the Driver (Prayer):

Lord, I am pulling over right now. Not because I am forced to. Because I am choosing to. I am choosing to stop the engine and just be still in Your presence. I do not come up with an agenda. I just need to rest. Restore what the road has taken out of me. Refill what has been emptied. Remind me why I am driving in the first place. I am not in a hurry right now. I am Yours. Amen.

---

[2] James Snyder, *In Pursuit of God: The Life of A.W. Tozer* (Camp Hill: Christian Publications, 1991), 114.

Chapter 10

The Fuel Gauge

(Running on Empty)

There is a moment every driver dread, the moment you look down and realize the needle is not just in the red, it is past it. You have been running on fumes. You do not know exactly when it happened because you have been so focused on the road ahead that you forgot to check the gauge.

This is what burnout looks like. It does not happen in a single moment. It is the result of miles and miles of ignoring the warning. The gauge drops slowly, first from full to half, then from half to a quarter, then to the red zone. At each stage, a wise driver would have stopped. But the driven man tells himself he can make it to the next exit.

When the engine finally dies on the side of the road, the driven man is always surprised. He should not be. God designed us with a gauge, our body, our spirit, our relationships all signal when the tank is low. The question is whether we have the humility to read it honestly and the wisdom to pull off before we are stranded.

The Map (Scripture):

> *"But he himself went a day's journey into the wilderness. He came to a broom bush, sat down under it and prayed that he might die. 'I have had enough, Lord,' he said." 1 Kings 19:4 (NIV)*

A Fellow Traveler: Elijah the Prophet

Elijah had just called down fire from heaven on Mount Carmel in one of the most dramatic displays of divine power in all of Scripture. He had stood alone against 450 prophets of Baal and won. And then, one threatening letter from Queen Jezebel later, he ran into the wilderness and asked God to let him die. This is not a story of a weak man. This is the story of a man who had given everything, a man whose fuel tank had been completely emptied in the service of God and who had no reserves left. God did not rebuke Elijah for his exhaustion. He sent an angel who touched him and said, "Get up and eat, because the journey is too great for you." God's response to burnout is not a sermon. It is bread, water, and rest. Elijah was refueled and went on to complete his assignment. The fuel gauge is not your enemy. It is God's mercy.

The Rearview Mirror (Reflections):

1. Where is your fuel gauge right now honestly? Full, half, quarter, red zone?
2. What has been draining your tank without you refilling it? Ministry, work, family pressure, unresolved conflict?
3. What would it look like to let God be your fuel station this week instead of running on your own reserves?

Talk to the Driver (Prayer):

God, I have been running on empty and pretending I was not. I am pulling over right now and admitting that my tank is empty. I need You to refuel me — not with more activity or achievement, but with Your presence and Your peace. I am done trying to run on fumes. Fill me up. I am not moving until You do.
Amen.

Chapter 11

The Reckless Driver

(Anger, Impulse, and the Cost of Lost Control)

There is a driver on every highway who terrifies everyone around him. He changes lanes without signaling, tailgates without mercy, and uses his vehicle as a weapon of intimidation. He is not driving toward anything. He is running from something inside himself. His anger has become the engine. The road is just the place he burns it.

Many men drive this way through life. The anger may have started as a defense — a wall built around a wound that was never treated. Over time, though, that wall became a weapon. The man who was once hurt became the man who hurts others. He damages every relationship he enters, leaves wreckage on every road he travels, and wonders why he is always alone at the destination.

The reckless driver is not beyond reach. But he cannot be reached until he is willing to stop the car, step out, and admit that his driving has been dangerous. The anger that fuels him is a signal — not a strategy. It is a check engine light pointing to a wound that the Master Mechanic is ready and willing to heal, if only the driver will let him under the hood.

The Map (Scripture):

> *"Be angry, and do not sin: do not let the sun go down on your wrath, nor give place to the devil." — Ephesians 4:26-27 (NKJV)*

A Fellow Traveler: Louis Zamperini

Louis Zamperini was an Olympic runner and a World War II hero who survived 47 days on a raft and years in a brutal Japanese POW camp. But when he came home, he brought a deep, unhealed wound with him. His trauma turned into explosive rage. He became a reckless driver in his own life—drinking heavily, fighting, and driving his marriage straight toward a cliff. His anger was the engine, and revenge was the only destination he could see. In 1949, facing a divorce, his wife convinced him to attend a Billy Graham crusade in Los Angeles. That night, Zamperini finally stopped the car. He surrendered his life to Christ, and the Master Mechanic did something impossible: He entirely removed the anger. Zamperini spent the rest of his life traveling the world to preach the Gospel and personally forgiving the very guards who had tortured him. The reckless driver was healed the moment he let God under the hood.

The Rearview Mirror (Reflections):

1. Is there any anger in you that has been driving your decisions? Where did it come from?

2. Who has been hurt by your "reckless driving", your spouse, your children, your colleagues?

3. What would it look like to hand the anger over to God today, not to suppress it, but to let Him heal the wound beneath it?

Talk to the Driver (Prayer):

Father, I must confess something I do not say out loud very often — I am angry. And I have been angry for a long time. I do not want the anger to keep driving my life. I am bringing it to You right now. I am not suppressing it, I am surrendering it. Heal what is underneath it. Replace the rage with something that will not destroy everything I touch. I need You to do what I cannot do for myself. In the name of Jesus Christ, who is the only One who can truly set a man free. Amen.

Chapter 12

The Passenger Seat

(Marriage as Partnership, Not Cargo)

In the early miles of marriage, we often make a critical error: we treat our wife like a passenger rather than a co-driver. She is in the car, yes. She is along for the journey. But the map is in our hands, the wheel is under our control, and her role we have unconsciously decided is to be grateful for the ride. That is not partnership. That is cargo management. And the woman God gave you was not designed to be cargo. She was designed to be the person who sees what you cannot see from the driver's seat, who reads the map when your eyes are on the road, who reminds you of the destination when you are tempted to take the exit that leads nowhere.

The men whose marriages survive the long road are the ones who learn sometimes painfully to turn to the passenger seat and say, "What do you see?" Your wife is not a backseat driver. She is a gift from God sitting right beside you. It is time to start driving like it.

The Map (Scripture):

> *"He who finds a wife finds a good thing, and obtains favor from the Lord." — Proverbs 18:22 (NKJV)*

A Fellow Traveler: Tony Evans

Dr. Tony Evans is one of the most respected Bible teachers in America, founder of Oak Cliff Bible Fellowship in Dallas and the Urban Alternative ministry that reaches millions globally. But Tony Evans has been transparent about the fact that for much of his early ministry, he treated his wife Lois as secondary to the mission. The ministry was the priority. The family — including Lois — was expected to support the vision without necessarily being included in shaping it. It was Lois who challenged Tony to align his private life with his public message. When Lois was diagnosed with cancer and passed away in 2019, Tony publicly acknowledged that she had been the true foundation of everything he had built. "She was the real hero," he said at her funeral.[3] The man who teaches millions about the Kingdom had to learn, through loss, that the passenger sitting beside him had been holding up his road the entire time.

The Rearview Mirror (Reflections):

1. Does your wife feel like a co-driver or like cargo? How do you know?
2. When was the last time you asked her, "What do you see?", and then actually listened without defending yourself?
3. What is one thing you can do this week to move her from the back seat to the passenger seat of your life?

Talk to the Driver (Prayer):

Lord, I want to be honest about my marriage today. There are ways I have treated my wife like cargo instead of a co-driver, and I know it. I have made decisions without her. I have dismissed what she sees. Forgive me. Help me become the husband who turns to his wife and actually listens. Help me honor the gift You gave me. Help me drive in a way that makes her grateful to be in the car. Amen.

---

[3] Tony Evans, eulogy for Lois Evans, Oak Cliff Bible Fellowship, Dallas, TX, December 30, 2019. Widely reported in Christian media.

Chapter 13

The Back Seat

(Fathering Well on the Long Road)

There is no greater responsibility a man carries in his vehicle than the passengers in the back seat. Children do not choose the car they are born into. They do not choose the driver. They arrive trusting that the person behind the wheel knows where he is going and will get them there safely. That trust is sacred.

The tragedy of fatherlessness — whether physical absence or emotional distance is that the back seat passengers are left to navigate alone. They watch the road ahead without a guide, learn to drive by watching a man who was never taught well himself, and carry the wounds of the journey long after they have their own vehicles.

But the road is not over. The driven man who discovers that he has been neglecting his back seat passengers still has miles ahead. The most powerful thing a father can do is not to pretend the distance never happened — it is to stop the car, open the back door, look his children in the eye, and say, "I see you. I am here. And from this mile forward, you have my full attention."

The Map (Scripture):

> *"And you, fathers, do not provoke your children to wrath, but bring them up in the training and admonition of the Lord." — Ephesians 6:4 (NKJV)*

A Fellow Traveler: Josh McDowell

Josh McDowell grew up in a home defined by his father's violent alcoholism. The abuse was severe and the wounds were deep. By his own account, he entered adulthood full of rage and determined to prove his worth through achievement. But after his conversion to Christianity and his subsequent decades of ministry to young people, McDowell made a deliberate and documented decision to become the father he never had. He has spoken publicly about investing intentionally in his four children, about being present, about breaking the cycle that his father drove him through. "I determined that my children would never question whether their father loved them," he has said.[4] [4]Josh McDowell is proof that the pattern can be broken — that a man who was left alone in the back seat can become the driver who never lets his own children feel that way.

The Rearview Mirror (Reflections):

1. What are your children learning about life, faith, and manhood simply by watching you drive?
2. Is there distance between you and one of your children that you have been avoiding? What is one step toward closing it?
3. What kind of driver do you want your children to remember when they are grown and have their own vehicles?

Talk to the Driver (Prayer):

Father, my children are watching the way I drive. Give me the courage to stop the car, open the back door, and look my kids in the eye. Give me the words to say what needs to be said. Help me become the father who shows up, not just physically, but fully present and fully invested. My children deserve a driver who knows where he is going. Help me be that man. Amen.

---

[4] Josh McDowell, *The Father Connection: How You Can Make the Difference in Your Child's Life* (Nashville: B&H Publishing, 2008), 47.

Chapter 14

The Carpool

(Brotherhood, Accountability, and the Men Who Keep You on the Road)

No man was built to drive alone. This is one of the great lies the driven man believes, that self-sufficiency is a virtue, that needing other men is a weakness, that the lone driver on an empty highway is the picture of strength. It is not. It is the picture of isolation. And isolated men make the worst decisions.

The carpool is not a compromise of your independence. It is a protection of it. The men who share your vehicle, your brothers in faith, your accountability partners, your trusted friends, they are the ones who will tell you when you are drifting, when your eyes are closing, when the exit you are about to take leads somewhere you promised you would never go again.

Every man who has finished the road well had other men in the car with him. Not passengers who praised his driving regardless of how reckless it was, but brothers who loved him enough to grab the wheel when necessary. Find your carpool. Open the door. Let them in.

The Map (Scripture):

> *"As iron sharpens iron, so a man sharpens the countenance of his friend." — Proverbs 27:17 (NKJV)*

A Fellow Traveler: Dietrich Bonhoeffer

In 1935, as the Nazi regime tightened its grip on Germany, Dietrich Bonhoeffer established an underground seminary at Finkenwalde. What he created there was not just a school, it was a carpool. A community of men who ate together, prayed together, confessed to one another, and held each other accountable in the most dangerous environment imaginable. His book Life Together remains one of the most powerful documents on Christian community ever produced. "The person who comes into a fellowship because he is running away from himself is misusing it for the sake of diversion,"[5] he wrote. Real brotherhood is not an escape from difficulty it is the place where men face difficulty together. Bonhoeffer was executed by the Nazis in April 1945, just days before the war ended. But the men who drove with him carried the road forward. The carpool outlasted the persecution.

The Rearview Mirror (Reflections):

1. Do you have men in your life who are honest enough to tell you when you are driving dangerously? If not, why not?
2. Is there a man in your circle right now who is drifting and needs someone to grab the wheel?
3. What would it take for you to open the door and let other men into the real journey not just the highlight reel?

Talk to the Driver (Prayer):

God, I have been driving alone when I did not have to. I am asking You to bring the right men into my life, men who will tell me the truth and stay in the car when things get hard. And give me the courage to open the door and let them in. I cannot finish this road alone. I was not designed to. Amen.

---

[5] Dietrich Bonhoeffer, *Life Together*, trans. John W. Doberstein (New York: HarperOne, 1954), 26.

Chapter 15

The Speed Trap

(Pride, Power, and the Fall That Follows)

Every highway has at least one speed trap. The road opens up, the scenery is beautiful, the engine is humming, and the driver begins to believe that the rules of the road no longer apply to him. He is moving too well, achieving too much, receiving too much praise for the ordinary speed limits to be relevant. He accelerates.

This is the speed trap. And it is not set by the enemy, it is set by the driver himself. Pride is not a sudden failure. It is a gradual acceleration that feels like success. Every compliment, every promotion, every moment of recognition adds a little more pressure to the pedal until the man is driving at a speed that makes correction impossible.

The speed trap does not discriminate. It catches generals and pastors, kings and businessmen, the powerful and the celebrated. The only protection against it is the daily discipline of humility, checking your speed not against the men around you, but against the Map.

The Map (Scripture):

> *"Pride goes before destruction, and a haughty spirit before a fall."*
> *— Proverbs 16:18 (NKJV)*

A Fellow Traveler: King David

David was a man after God's own heart — a warrior, a poet, a king, a worshipper. He had defeated Goliath as a boy and built a kingdom as a man. By the time he saw Bathsheba on the rooftop, he had been on the road long enough to believe that the speed limits no longer applied to him. Each step of his collapse was possible only because pride had been accelerating for years. The crash was catastrophic — a dead child, a murdered loyal soldier, a family torn apart by violence. But the most remarkable thing about David's story is not the speed trap — it is what happened after. Psalm 51 is one of the most honest pieces of writing in all of human history. A man who had driven at the speed of a god writing to the God who still loved him. The speed trap broke David. But the breaking made him real.

The Rearview Mirror (Reflections):

1. Where in your life are you currently accelerating past the speed limit?
2. What fuels that speed?
3. Is there someone in your life with the authority to pull you over? Have you given them that authority?
4. What would humility look like in the specific area where your speed is highest right now?

Talk to the Driver (Prayer):

Lord, I have been driving too fast and I have not been checking my speed. I am pulling over right now and asking You to recalibrate my heart. Strip away the pride that has been building without me noticing it. Remind me that every mile I have driven has been by Your grace, not my skill. Keep me humble. Keep me teachable. Keep me dependent on You. Amen.

Chapter 16

The Detour

(When God Reroutes Everything)

There are seasons when the road ahead simply closes. The orange cones appear without warning, the signs redirect you onto an unfamiliar path, and everything in you resists the detour. This was not the plan. This was not the route.

The detour feels like a delay. It feels like punishment, or worse, like God has lost the address. But the man of faith who looks back at his life from a distance will often see that the detour was not a deviation from the destination — it was the route to it. The pit was part of the journey. The prison was part of the preparation.

The detour demands something the highway does not: trust. On the highway, you can see for miles. On the detour, you can only see the next turn. God does not always explain the detour. He simply asks you to follow the signs, trust the Navigator, and keep moving forward.

The Map (Scripture):

> *"But as for you, you meant evil against me; but God meant it for good, in order to bring it about as it is this day, to save many people alive." — Genesis 50:20 (NKJV)*

A Fellow Traveler: Joseph

Joseph's journey is the most documented detour in Scripture. Thrown into a pit by his brothers, sold into slavery, falsely accused, forgotten in prison for years, every mile of his road looked like a wrong turn. There was no visible highway. There were no signs pointing to the palace. Yet when Joseph stood before his brothers as the second most powerful man in Egypt, he was able to say with absolute clarity: this was the route. Every pit, every chain, every forgotten promise was a construction zone preparing the road he was always destined to travel. Joseph did not understand the detour while he was in it. He trusted the Mapmaker while he could not read the Map. That is the definition of faith on the road.

The Rearview Mirror (Reflections):

1. What detour are you currently on that you did not choose and do not understand.
2. Looking back at your road, can you identify a detour that turned out to be the route?
3. What would it look like to trust God's navigation in this season, even when you cannot see the next turn?

Talk to the Driver (Prayer):

Father, this detour I am on right now does not make sense to me. I had a plan and now the road is closed. I am not going to pretend I am okay with it. But I am choosing to trust You anyway. I believe You can see the road ahead even when I cannot. Navigate me through this. I am following Your signs, even when I do not understand them. Amen.

Chapter 17

The Pit Stop

(Discipline, Maintenance, and Running to Win)

In competitive racing, the pit stop is not optional. It is strategic. The driver who refuses to stop for tires and fuel because he does not want to lose his position will lose the race entirely — not because he lacked speed, but because he lacked the discipline to maintain the vehicle.

Spiritual discipline works the same way. Prayer is a pit stop. Scripture is a pit stop. Fasting, solitude, worship, and confession, these are all pit stops. The driven man who dismisses them as inefficient or impractical is the man who will find his vehicle falling apart at the worst possible moment.

The most dangerous driver on the road is not the reckless one. It is the man who was once disciplined, who let his disciplines slip so gradually he never noticed how bad things had gotten. The pit stop is not a pause in the journey, it is the reason the journey continues.

The Map (Scripture):

> *"And everyone who competes for the prize is temperate in all things. Now they do it to obtain a perishable crown, but we for an imperishable crown." 1 Corinthians 9:25 (NKJV)*

A Fellow Traveler: Eric Liddell

Eric Liddell was one of the fastest men on earth in 1924. A Scottish sprinter and deeply committed Christian, he was the favorite to win the 100 meters at the Paris Olympics. When he discovered that the qualifying heats were scheduled for a Sunday, he withdrew from his best event without hesitation. The Sabbath was a non-negotiable pit stop. His coaches, his country, and the Prince of Wales pressured him to reconsider. He did not. He entered the 400 meters instead not his specialty trained relentlessly and won the gold medal in a world record time. His story, immortalized in Chariots of[6]Fire, is about a man who understood that the disciplines of faith were not obstacles to his performance were the foundation of it. Liddell went on to serve as a missionary in China, where he died in a Japanese internment camp in 1945. Those who knew him there said he ran the same race in the camp that he had run on the track with everything, for the glory of God.

The Rearview Mirror (Reflections):

1. What spiritual disciplines have you been skipping because you feel too busy?
2. What is the condition of your vehicle right now, honestly what maintenance has been deferred?
3. What would it look like to build one non-negotiable pit stop into every day this week?

Talk to the Driver (Prayer):

God, I have been skipping the pit stops and telling myself I do not have time for them. And I can feel it in my driving. I am coming back to the pit stop right now. Help me build these disciplines into my life not as religious obligations but as the fuel that keeps me running. I cannot drive well without them. I know that now. Amen.

[6] Sally Magnusson, *The Flying Scotsman: A Biography* (New York: Quartet Books, 1981), 98.

Chapter 18

The Blind Spot

(What We Refuse to See)

Every vehicle has a blind spot — a zone just outside the range of the mirrors where danger hides invisible to the driver. Most collisions do not happen because the driver saw the danger and ignored it. They happened because the driver genuinely did not see it.

The moral blind spot works exactly this way. It is not the obvious temptation that destroys most men — it is the one they cannot see. The rationalization that has been in place so long no longer looks like a rationalization. The compromise that has been normalized so thoroughly it no longer feels like a compromise.

The only way to address a blind spot is to create systems around it — other drivers who will warn you, regular checks of your own mirrors, and the humility to believe that your vision is not as complete as you think it is.

The Map (Scripture):

> *"Search me, O God, and know my heart; try me, and know my anxieties; and see if there is any wicked way in me, and lead me in the way everlasting." — Psalm 139:23-24 (NKJV)*

A Fellow Traveler: Chuck Colson

Chuck Colson was one of the most powerful men in Washington during the Nixon administration, he was known as Nixon's "hatchet man." By his own later admission, he had a massive blind spot: he had convinced himself that the ends justified the means, that loyalty to the President was the highest virtue, and that the normal rules of ethical conduct did not apply to men operating at his level. Watergate did not create Colson's blind spot, it exposed it. His conversion to Christianity in

1973 was the moment he finally looked into the blind spot and saw himself clearly. Colson went on to found Prison Fellowship, one of the largest prison ministry organizations in the world, spending the rest of his life using the very access and influence he had once misused in service of men behind bars. The blind spot, once seen, became his mission field.

The Rearview Mirror (Reflections):

1. What is the area of your life that you are most resistant to having examined? That resistance is often the location of the blind spot.
2. Who in your life has the access and the trust to tell you what you cannot see about yourself?
3. Have you given God permission to show you your blind spots?

Talk to the Driver (Prayer):

Lord, I am asking You to show me my blind spots. The areas I cannot see. The rationalizations I have accepted so long they feel like truth. I am giving You permission to turn on the lights in the dark corners of my life and show me what is there. I trust that You will not show me what You are not ready to help me address. Search me. Know me. Lead me in the way everlasting. Amen.

Chapter 19

The Construction Zone

(Patience When the Road Is Torn Up)

Then there are seasons when the open highway narrows into a construction zone without warning. The lanes narrow. The speed drops. The orange barrels stretch for miles with no visible end. You cannot see the progress being made. All you can see is the disruption, the delay, and the distance you are not covering.

God's construction zones are among the most disorienting experiences a man can pass through. A season of waiting. A closed door where an open one was expected. A promise that is taking far longer to be fulfilled than the map suggested.

But the construction zone is not punishment. It is preparation. The road that is being torn up and rebuilt will carry greater weight when it is finished. The foundation that is being laid in the season of waiting will hold what is coming. The flagman is not your enemy. He is standing between you and a road your vehicle is not ready for.

The Map (Scripture):

> *"But those who wait on the Lord shall renew their strength; they shall mount up with wings like eagles, they shall run and not be weary, they shall walk and not faint." — Isaiah 40:31 (NKJV)*

A Fellow Traveler: Nelson Mandela

Nelson Mandela spent 27 years in Robben Island prison for his opposition to the apartheid regime in South Africa. By any measure, those years were a construction zone — a period of enforced waiting that most men would not have survived with their spirit intact. Yet when he emerged in 1990, those who knew him before and after said the same thing: the prison had not broken him. It had built him. The impatience and reactiveness of the young Mandela had been replaced by a patience, wisdom, and capacity for forgiveness that the world had never seen in a political leader. He became the first democratically elected President of South Africa in 1994 and led his nation away from civil war through reconciliation that stunned the world. The construction zone had been doing something that the open highway never could. It built the man the road required.

The Rearview Mirror (Reflections):

1. What construction zone are you currently in — a season of waiting, a closed door, a promise delayed?
2. What is God possibly building in you during this season that could not be built any other way?
3. What would it look like to cooperate with the construction instead of fighting it?

Talk to the Driver (Prayer):

Father, I am in a construction zone and I do not like it. I am impatient and I want to be moving. But I am choosing today to trust that the road You are building in this season is worth the wait. I will not try to force my way through. I will wait on You and trust that what You are building is better than anything I could build on my own. Amen.

Chapter 20

The Hitchhiker

(Carrying Those Who Cannot Drive Themselves)

Not everyone on the road has a vehicle. They were never given one, or the one they had broke down beyond their ability to repair it, or someone took it from them. They are standing on the shoulder with their thumb out, hoping that someone with enough room and enough compassion will stop. Most drivers keep going.

The man who has been restored has a responsibility to the hitchhiker. The body shop, the new GPS, the purposeful drive toward the Eternal City none of that was just for him. Not to carry everyone indefinitely. But to recognize that the road he is travelling on was made possible by the grace of someone who stopped for him when he was stranded.

The man who stops for the hitchhiker is not losing time. He is spending it on something that matters. The road to the Eternal City passes directly through the lives of people who need what you have.

The Map (Scripture):

> *"Carry each other's burdens, and in this way you will fulfill the law of Christ." — Galatians 6:2 (NIV)*

A Fellow Traveler: William Wilberforce

William Wilberforce was a gifted young politician in 18th century Britain — charming, wealthy, socially connected, and destined for a comfortable ride to the top of English political life. His conversion to evangelical Christianity in 1785 redirected it entirely toward the hitchhikers on the road — specifically, the millions of Africans being trafficked in chains across the Atlantic Ocean. Wilberforce spent 46 years in Parliament fighting for the abolition of the slave trade and slavery itself, enduring defeat after defeat, mockery, illness, and threats to his life. The Slavery Abolition Act passed through Parliament in 1833. Wilberforce died three days later, as if he had been sustained by the road itself until the final mile was complete. He gave his entire vehicle — his talent, his platform, his health, his years — to people he would never meet, who could never repay him.

The Rearview Mirror (Reflections):

1. Who are the hitchhikers in your immediate world? People with no vehicle who need someone to stop?

2. What has God given you talent, platform, resources, experience that was meant to carry others, not just yourself?

3. Is there a cause or a person that God has been placing on your road consistently? What would it look like to stop and make room?

Talk to the Driver (Prayer):

God, open my eyes to the people on the side of the road that I have been driving past. Show me who needs me to stop. Give me the generosity to make room, even when it is inconvenient. Remind me that I was once stranded too, and someone stopped for me. Let me be that person for someone else today.
Amen.

Chapter 21

The Foggy Road

(Walking by Faith When Visibility Is Zero)

Some mornings you get in the vehicle and cannot see ten feet ahead. The fog is total. The road is familiar, but it is invisible. Every instinct says to stop — to wait until the conditions improve, until the path is clear, until you can see where you are going before you commit to going there.

But the fog does not always lift on command. There are seasons of life when the visibility is zero and the road must still be traveled. The man whose faith is contingent on clear conditions will never reach the destination — because the destination was always on the other side of the fog.

Driving in fog requires a completely different approach. You slow down. You stay close to the lines. You listen more than you look. You trust that the road is there even when you cannot see it. That is faith in its purest form. Not the absence of fear, but the choice to keep moving forward anyway.

The Map (Scripture):

"For we walk by faith, not by sight." 2 Corinthians 5:7 (NKJV)

A Fellow Traveler: Corrie ten Boom

Corrie ten Boom was a Dutch watchmaker's daughter who hid Jewish refugees in her home during the Nazi occupation of the Netherlands. In 1944, she and her family were arrested and sent to concentration camps. Her beloved sister Betsie died at Ravensbrück. Corrie survived. She emerged from one of the darkest roads in human history not with bitterness, but with a message she spent the rest of her life delivering across the world: "There is no pit so deep that God's love is not deeper still."[7] Corrie did not have visibility in the camp. She could not understand why God would allow what was happening. She drove by faith alone. And what she discovered in the fog became the most powerful testimony of the 20th century. She drove that fog-covered road all the way to the Eternal City, arriving on her 91st birthday in 1983.

The Rearview Mirror (Reflections):

1. What is the fog in your current season? The area where you have no visibility and cannot see the road ahead?

2. What does "driving by faith" look like practically in your situation right now? What is the next ten feet you can see?

3. Has God been faithful to you in past fogs? What does that history tell you about the fog you are in now?

Talk to the Driver (Prayer):

Lord, I cannot see the road ahead right now and I am scared. But I am not stopping. I am choosing to trust that You laid this road, and You know every curve that is coming. I am slowing down. I am listening for Your voice. I am staying close to the lines of Your Word. Lead me through this fog. I am driving by faith in You today. Amen.

---

[7] Corrie ten Boom, John Sherrill, and Elizabeth Sherrill, *The Hiding Place* (Old Tappan: Chosen Books, 1971), 217.

Chapter 22

The Road Hazard

(Spiritual Warfare and the Enemy on the Highway)

Not everything on the road is accidental. There is an enemy who has studied your route, knows exactly where you are weakest, and times his moves accordingly. The blowout that happens when you are already running late. The distraction that appears at the moment of your greatest focus.

The man who does not believe in spiritual warfare is the most exposed driver on the road. He attributes every hazard to coincidence, every setback to bad luck, never recognizing that there is an intelligence behind the obstacles designed to stop him before he reaches his destination.

But the man of faith is not defenseless. He has armor designed specifically for the road — truth, righteousness, faith, salvation, the Word of God. These are not decorative. They are functional. The man who puts them on every morning before he starts the engine is the man who arrives at the destination.

The Map (Scripture):

> *"Put on the full armor of God, so that you can take your stand against the devil's schemes." — Ephesians 6:11 (NIV)*

A Fellow Traveler: Martin Luther

On October 31, 1517, Martin Luther nailed 95 Theses to the door of the Castle Church in Wittenberg, Germany, and triggered a road hazard that nearly destroyed him. The most powerful religious institution in the Western world turned its full force against him — excommunication, condemnation, threats of execution. Luther's response at the Diet of Worms, "Here I stand. I can do no other. God help me."[8] is one of the most famous declarations of a man who saw the hazards clearly and drove straight through them anyway. He was prepared. He understood that the road he was traveling was contested, and that the only protection available to him was the Word of God and the conviction that He who had called him would not abandon him. Luther was protected, hidden at the Wartburg Castle, and went on to translate the Bible into German and change the course of Western civilization. The road hazard is real. So is the armor.

The Rearview Mirror (Reflections):

1. What road hazards have appeared in your life recently that seem designed specifically for your vulnerabilities?

2. Are you wearing the full armor of God daily, or are you driving spiritually unprotected?

3. What is the one area of your road where you are most exposed right now, and what specific piece of armor do you need to put on?

Talk to the Driver (Prayer):

Father, I know there is an enemy on this road, and I have not always taken him seriously. Right now, I am putting on every piece of armor You have given me truth, righteousness, faith, salvation, and Your Word. I am not driving into today unequipped. Give me discernment to recognize the enemy strategy before it takes me off the road. I am fighting with You, not alone. Amen.

---

[8] Roland H. Bainton, *Here I Stand: A Life of Martin Luther* (New York: Abingdon-Cokesbury Press, 1950), 185.

Chapter 23

The Engine Overhaul

(Total Surrender and the New Heart)

There comes a moment in every restoration story when the Master Mechanic delivers a diagnosis that the driver is not prepared for. It is not a tune-up that is needed. It is not new tires or fresh oil. The engine itself must be replaced. The problem is not on the surface. It is at the core.

That is the moment of total surrender. It is the moment when a man stops negotiating with God about which parts of himself, he is willing to give up and begins to understand that the offer on the table is not partial renovation — it is complete transformation. A new heart. A new engine. A new man.

The resistance to total surrender is the greatest obstacle on the road to restoration. We want the benefits of the new engine without giving up the old one. But the Master Mechanic will not install a new engine in a vehicle whose driver is still revving the old one. Total surrender is not the end of who you are. It is the beginning of who you were always meant to be.

The Map (Scripture):

> *"I will give you a new heart and put a new spirit within you; I will take the heart of stone out of your flesh and give you a heart of flesh." — Ezekiel 36:26 (NKJV)*

A Fellow Traveler: Augustine of Hippo

Augustine of Hippo is one of the most intellectually brilliant figures in the history of Christianity. His autobiography, Confessions, written in the 4th century, contains one of the most famous prayers in history:

"Lord, make me chaste — but not yet."[9] For years, Augustine drove at full speed on the road of intellectual achievement and pleasure, knowing that the life he was living was not the life he was made for, but unable to fully release the wheel. His mother Monica prayed for him for 33 years. And finally, in a garden in Milan in 386 AD, Augustine heard a child's voice saying, "Take up and read," opened Paul's letter to the Romans, and the engine overhauled. He surrendered completely. The man who had prayed "not yet" became the man who wrote The City of God, one of the most influential books in the history of Western civilization. The overhaul that he resisted for decades produced a vehicle that carried the Gospel for centuries.

The Rearview Mirror (Reflections):

1. What part of yourself have you been keeping back from God — the area where your prayer has been "change me, but not that part"?

2. What would total surrender look like in your specific situation? What would you have to release?

3. Do you believe that God's new engine is better than the one you have been running on?

Talk to the Driver (Prayer):

God, I have been holding something back and You know what it is. I have been willing to let You fix the dents but not replace the engine. Today I am done negotiating. I am surrendering it completely — the part I have been protecting, the part I have been afraid to give up. Take it. Replace it with something new. I trust the Mechanic. Do the full overhaul. Amen.

---

[9] Augustine of Hippo, *Confessions*, trans. Henry Chadwick (Oxford: Oxford University Press, 1991), 8.7.17.

Chapter 24

The Co-Driver

(Learning to Yield to the Holy Spirit)

After the engine overhaul, something remarkable happens. There is a new presence in the car, a Co-Driver who has always been available but was never given the seat. The Holy Spirit does not force His way into the driver's seat. He waits. He counsels. He illuminates the road ahead. But He will only lead the man who is willing to follow.

Learning to yield to the Holy Spirit is one of the most counterintuitive skills a driven man can develop. He has spent his entire life trusting his own instincts, his own experience, his own assessment of the road. Now he is being asked to follow a voice that does not always explain itself.

But the man who learns to yield discovers something that changes everything: the Codriver is never wrong. Every prompt that was followed and every warning that was heeded leads to outcomes that confirm the trustworthiness of the voice. The Co-Driver is not a limitation. He is the greatest advantage on the road.

The Map (Scripture):

> *"However, when He, the Spirit of truth, has come, He will guide you into all truth." — John 16:13 (NKJV)*

A Fellow Traveler: Smith Wigglesworth

Smith Wigglesworth was a plumber from Bradford, England, who could barely read when he was baptized in the Holy Spirit in 1907. By every natural measure, he had nothing to offer Christian ministry. But he became one of the most remarkable figures in 20th century

Christianity, traveling the world with a ministry marked by extraordinary results, simply because he learned to yield completely to the prompting of the Spirit. His theology was not complex: "Only believe."[10] He was simply a man who learned that the Co-Driver was more reliable than any navigation he could produce on his own. He drove until he was 87 years old, in full ministry, and died in 1947 after preaching at a friend's funeral. The Co-Driver navigated every mile.

The Rearview Mirror (Reflections):

1. What has the Holy Spirit been prompting you to do, say, or stop that you have been overriding with your own logic?
2. What would it look like to spend one day this week actively listening for the Spirit's direction before making your own plans?
3. What is the greatest evidence in your life so far that the Co-Driver's navigation is more reliable than your own?

Talk to the Driver (Prayer):

Holy Spirit, I have been overriding Your prompts with my own logic for too long. I am sorry. Today I am asking You to take the Co-Driver seat and I am committing to follow Your direction, even when it does not make sense to me.
I trust You more than I trust myself. Lead me. I am yielding. Amen.

---

[10] Stanley Howard Frodsham, *Smith Wigglesworth: Apostle of Faith* (Springfield: Gospel Publishing House, 1948), 72.

Chapter 25

The Toll Road

(The Cost of Discipleship and the Road Worth Paying For)

Not all roads are free. Some of the most important roads in the journey — the ones that lead to the most significant destinations — require a toll. There is a cost at the gate, and the driver must decide before he passes through whether the destination is worth the price of admission.

Discipleship is a toll road. Following Christ does not cost nothing — it costs everything. The comfort of fitting in with the culture. The security of a life built entirely around self-protection. The approval of people who will not understand your new direction. These are the tolls. They are real.

But the toll road leads somewhere the free road cannot go. The man who pays the toll always discovers the same thing: what he gave up was worth far less than what he found on the other side. The toll is not a punishment. Think of it as a filter. It separates the men who are serious about the destination from the men who just wanted to drive.

The Map (Scripture):

> *"Then he said to them all: 'Whoever wants to be my disciple must deny themselves and take up their cross daily and follow me.'" — Luke 9:23 (NIV)*

A Fellow Traveler: Jim Elliot

Jim Elliot was a young American missionary who, in January 1956, flew a small plane into the jungle of Ecuador to make contact with the Waodani people — a tribe known for their violence. He was 28 years old. He was speared to death on a riverbank, along with four other missionaries. His journal contained the words that have since become one of the most quoted statements in the history of Christian missions: "He is no fool who gives what he cannot keep to gain what he cannot lose."[11] Elliot understood the toll road. He drove up to the gate knowing exactly what it would cost and paid it without hesitation. The story did not end at the riverbank. His wife Elisabeth returned to live among the Waodani people. The tribe that killed Jim Elliot was eventually reached with the Gospel. The man who baptized Jim Elliot's daughter years later was one of the men who had held the spear. The toll road led somewhere the free road never could.

The Rearview Mirror (Reflections):

1. What toll is God asking you to pay right now in your journey of discipleship?
2. What have you already paid on the toll road that has proven to be worth the cost?
3. Is there a road you are avoiding because you know it will require more than you feel ready to give? What is waiting on the other side of that gate?

Talk to the Driver (Prayer):

Lord, You are asking me to pay a toll that I have been avoiding. I can see the gate and I know what it will cost. Today I am driving up to it. I am paying what is required. I am trusting that the road on the other side is worth every sacrifice this side demands. Here is the toll. I am going through. Amen.

---

[11] Jim Elliot, *The Journals of Jim Elliot*, ed. Elisabeth Elliot (Old Tappan: Fleming H. Revell, 1978), entry for October 28, 1949.

Chapter 26

The Legacy Lane

(What You Leave Behind on the Road)

Every driver leaves something on the road behind him. The question is not whether you will leave a legacy, the question is what kind. Some men leave skid marks, the evidence of emergency stops, close calls, and lives disrupted by the chaos of their driving. Some leave nothing at all.

But the man who drives by the Map, who carries his passengers well, who stops for the hitchhiker and maintains his vehicle and yields to the Co-Driver, this man leaves a road behind him that others can follow. His tire tracks are a trail. His story is a map. His life is proof that the destination is real.

Legacy is not about being remembered. It is about being useful long after you are gone. Every life that is touched, every truth that is spoken, every act of faithfulness in obscurity, these are the mile markers of a legacy that outlasts the driver.

The Map (Scripture):

> *"A good person leaves an inheritance for their children's children."*
> *— Proverbs 13:22 (NIV)*

A Fellow Traveler: John Newton

John Newton was a slave trader. He captained ships that transported hundreds of human beings across the Atlantic in conditions of unimaginable suffering. His conversion came during a violent storm at sea in 1748, when he cried out to God in terror and found, to his astonishment, that God answered. Eventually he left the sea, became an ordained minister, and spent the rest of his life in service to the God who had rescued him. He wrote "Amazing Grace" as an autobiographical testimony — the wretch who had been found. In his final years, he became a crucial witness in the parliamentary campaign to abolish the slave trade, testifying before Parliament about the horrors he had participated in. He died in 1807, the same year the British slave trade was abolished. His legacy outlived every mile of his road. The song he wrote from the wreckage of his life is still sung in every language on earth.

The Rearview Mirror (Reflections):

1. What do you want people to say about your driving when your road is finished?
2. What are you currently doing that will matter in 50 years? In 100 years?
3. What is the most important thing you can pass on to the next generation — not of wealth, but of road wisdom?

Talk to the Driver (Prayer):

Father, I want to leave something behind on this road that matters. Not just achievements or a name — but a trail that points people toward You. Help me live in a way that creates a legacy worth following. Let my tire tracks be a map that the next generation can use to find their way to the Eternal City. Make everything I have been through useful for someone who comes after me.
Amen.

Chapter 27

Passing the Keys

(Mentoring the Next Driver)

At some point, the most valuable thing a man can do is not push harder himself. It stop long enough to teach someone else the road. The miles you have accumulated, the hard-won knowledge of the road, the lessons learned from collisions and detours and construction zones are not yours to keep. They are yours to give.

Mentorship is not a program or a checklist. It is a relationship. It is the experienced driver who pulls over, opens the passenger door, and says to a younger man, "Get in. I am going to show you the road."

The man who hoards his road wisdom, who believes that younger men should earn their knowledge the same hard way he did is the man whose legacy dies with him. But the man who passes the keys intentionally multiplies his impact beyond anything he could achieve alone.

The Map (Scripture):

> *"And the things that you have heard from me among many witnesses, commit these to faithful men who will be able to teach others also."*
>
> *2 Timothy 2:2 (NKJV)*

A Fellow Traveler: Paul and Timothy

The relationship between the Apostle Paul and young Timothy is the New Testament's definitive model of mentorship. Paul found Timothy in Lystra on his second missionary journey — a young man whose mother and grandmother had faithfully passed their faith to him. Paul saw something in Timothy that Timothy could not yet see in himself. He invited him to join the journey. He took him into dangerous cities. He wrote him letters that combined practical instruction with deep affection. He told him, "Don't let anyone look down on you because you are young, but set an example." Paul was passing the keys — not when he felt ready to retire, but in the middle of the most active period of his own ministry. Timothy went on to lead the church in Ephesus. The keys Paul passed became the foundation of a legacy that shaped Western civilization.

The Rearview Mirror (Reflections):

1. Who passed the keys to you — who invested in your road when you were young and unproven?
2. Who is in your life right now that needs you to pull over and open the passenger door?
3. What specific road wisdom do you have forged through your own miles that you have never intentionally passed on to anyone?

Talk to the Driver (Prayer):

God, somewhere there is a younger man who needs what I have learned on this road. Give me the humility to stop, open the door, and invite him in. Give me the patience to invest in someone who cannot repay me. Help me be the man that someone else needed and did not have. I am passing the keys. Show me who to give them to. Amen.

Chapter 28

The Homestretch

(Finishing Strong When the Road Grows Long)

The homestretch is deceptive. You can see the destination from here. The end of the road is visible. The temptation is to relax, to take the foot off the pedal, to stop checking the mirrors, to assume that because you are close, the remaining miles require less attention than the ones behind you.

History tells a different story. Many men who drove faithfully for decades made their worst decisions in the homestretch. The collision that destroyed what decades of faithful driving had built. The pride that crept in precisely because the destination was in sight.

Finishing strong is not the natural outcome of starting well. It is the result of deciding, every single day of the homestretch, to drive with the same discipline, the same humility, and the same dependence on the Map that carried you through the early miles.

The Map (Scripture):

> *"I have fought the good fight, I have finished the race, I have kept the faith." 2 Timothy 4:7 (NKJV)*

A Fellow Traveler: Billy Graham

Billy Graham preached the Gospel to more people in person than anyone in history — an estimated 215 million people across more than 185 countries over six decades of ministry. But what is perhaps most remarkable about Billy Graham is not the breadth of his impact it is the integrity of his homestretch. Early in his ministry he implemented what became known as "the Modesto Manifesto"[12], a set of personal accountability rules designed to protect him from the most common road hazards. He never traveled alone with a woman other than his wife. All finances were publicly accountable. Ego and self-promotion were deliberately avoided. These disciplines were not imposed on him. They were disciplines he chose because he understood that the road was long and the hazards were real. He died in 2018 at the age of 99, having finished the race with his integrity intact. The homestretch was as clean as the beginning.

The Rearview Mirror (Reflections):

1. What are the specific disciplines you have in place to protect you in the homestretch of your current season?

2. Is there an area where you have lowered your guard because you feel like you are close to the destination?

3. What does "finishing strong" look like for you specifically — in your marriage, your family, your faith, your work?

Talk to the Driver (Prayer):

Lord, I want to finish well. Not just start strong. I want to be the man who is still faithful, still humble, still pointing toward You in the final stretch. Guard me against the complacency that comes with distance traveled. Keep my character intact. And when I step out of this vehicle for the last time, let there be nothing left on the road that I wish I had done differently. Help me finish the way I want to be remembered. Amen.

---

[12] Billy Graham, *Just As I Am: The Autobiography of Billy Graham* (New York: HarperCollins, 1997), 128–132.

Chapter 29

The Rearview Mirror

(Gratitude for Every Mile)

As the Eternal City comes into view, a wise driver takes one long look in the rearview mirror. Not to live there, the road behind is not the destination. But to see it clearly. To count the miles. To remember the collisions and the detours and the construction zones and the passengers and the moments when the fuel gauge was empty and somehow, impossibly, you are still driving.

Gratitude is the discipline of looking in the rearview mirror and seeing grace. Not luck. Not skill. Just grace. Every mile that you should not have survived but did. Every relationship that should have been destroyed but was restored. Every wrong turn that became the route.

Arriving at the Eternal City without gratitude means missing the whole point of the road. The road was never about the destination alone. It was about the transformation that happened on the way. Every mile was a gift. Look in the mirror. Give thanks. Then drive the final stretch with everything you have.

The Map (Scripture):

> *"Give thanks in all circumstances; for this is God's will for you in Christ Jesus." 1 Thessalonians 5:18 (NIV)*

A Fellow Traveler: Johnny Cash

Johnny Cash's road is one of the most dramatic in the history of American music. The Arkansas farm boy who became the Man in Black drove through every hazard the highway offers — addiction to amphetamines and alcohol that nearly killed him multiple times, a first marriage destroyed by his absence and unfaithfulness, a period when his career collapsed alongside his body and his soul. But Cash's story did not end in the wreckage. His marriage to June Carter, his return to faith, and his later years were marked by a gratitude so raw and so genuine that it became the defining characteristic of his art. His final recordings — the American Recordings series — are perhaps the most honest music ever made by a man who knew he was near the end of the road. His cover of "Hurt"[13] became a monument to a man looking in the rearview mirror without flinching and giving thanks for the grace that had carried him through every mile of a road he had no right to survive. He died in September 2003, four months after June. The gratitude was the last thing he carried.

The Rearview Mirror (Reflections):
What mile of your road are you most grateful for — the one that hurt the most but built the most?
Is there someone who drove alongside you through a difficult season that you have never properly thanked?
What does your rearview mirror show you about the character and faithfulness of God across the length of your road?

Talk to the Driver (Prayer):
Father, today I am looking in the rearview mirror and I am choosing gratitude. Not because every mile was easy. But because You were faithful on every mile, even the ones I drove badly. Thank You for the collisions that woke me up. Thank You for the detours that built me. Thank You for not giving up on me when I gave You every reason to. Every mile was a gift. Even the hard ones. Especially the hard ones. Amen.

---

[13] Steve Turner, *The Man Called Cash: The Life, Love, and Faith of an American Legend* (Nashville: W Publishing Group, 2004), 201–204.

Chapter 30

The Final Mile

(Arriving Well at the Eternal City)

Every road has a final mile. Every engine stops. One day, every driver steps out of the vehicle for the last time. This is not a tragedy — it is the completion of the journey. The destination was never the road. The destination was always the City at the end of it.

The final mile is the mile where everything unnecessary falls away. The titles don't matter. The achievements don't matter. The balance in the account doesn't matter. What matters is this: Did you drive by the Map? Did you finish the race? Did you keep the faith? Did you love the people in your car? Did you stop for the hitchhiker? Did you pass the keys?

The Eternal City is not a reward for perfect driving. No one drove perfectly. It is the destination for every man who, despite the collisions and the wrong turns and the construction zones and the empty fuel tanks, kept saying yes to the Master Mechanic's offer of restoration and kept pointing the vehicle toward home. Drive the final mile with everything you have. And then get out of the car, look up, and hear the words every driver on this road has been working toward: 'Well done, good and faithful servant. Welcome home.'

The Map (Scripture):

> *"I have fought the good fight, I have finished the race, I have kept the faith. Finally, there is laid up for me the crown of righteousness, which the Lord, the righteous Judge, will give to me on that Day, and not to me only but also to all who have loved His appearing." 2 Timothy 4:7-8 (NKJV)*

A Fellow Traveler: The Apostle Paul

No driver in the history of the Church traveled a more eventful road than the Apostle Paul. He began as Saul of Tarsus — a man so committed to destroying the early followers of Jesus that he held the coats of the men who stoned Stephen to death. His encounter with the risen Christ on the road to Damascus was the most dramatic collision in history. What followed was thirty years of the most consequential driving in the history of Christianity — three missionary journeys across the Roman Empire, multiple imprisonments, shipwrecks, beatings, and a relentless movement toward the destination that nothing could stop. He wrote his final letter from a Roman prison cell, knowing his execution was imminent. And in it, he looked in the rearview mirror and said with complete confidence: I fought the good fight. I finished the race. I kept the faith. He did not arrive at the Eternal City by accident. He arrived because every mile had been driven in the same direction, toward the same destination, with the same Map. The final mile was simply the completion of a journey that had been pointed home from the very first day. Drive like Paul. Arrive like Paul.

The Rearview Mirror (Reflections):

If your road ended today, would you be able to say with confidence: I fought the good fight, I finished the race, I kept the faith?

What adjustments do you need to make right now to ensure that your final mile is driven in the right direction?

Who will you bring with you to the Eternal City — whose road are you directly influencing toward the destination?

Talk to the Driver (Prayer):

Lord, I want to arrive well. I want to cross the finish line with my faith intact, my family beside me, and my hands still on the wheel You placed them on. I do not need a perfect record. I just need Your grace to carry me the rest of the way. When I step out of this vehicle and stand before You, I want to hear those words — Well done. I am driving for that. I am living for that. See You at the Eternal City. Amen.

Author's Closing Message

The Long Road Home

If you are reading these words, it means you've taken the time to pull over. You've looked at your dashboard, you've checked your GPS, and perhaps you've even admitted that your "engine" needs the Master Mechanic's touch.

I wrote this because I know what it's like to hit the road at full speed. I know the thrill of the "Assembly Line" and the blinding fury of "Road Rage" when ambition takes the wheel. I've seen the wreckage of the "Collision" and felt the weight of trying to pick up the pieces alone.

But I also know the peace of the "Tow Truck." I know the quiet, steady hope of the "Body Shop" where God doesn't just fix our dents , He gives us a new heart. Keep your eyes on the Eternal City. Don't let the "Road Rage" of this world steal your joy, and don't let the "Wrong Turns" of your past keep you from your future.

I'll see you at the Final Destination.

Josmar Pereira

Epilogue

The journey doesn't end when you close this book; it begins when you put your hand back on the wheel with a new Navigator. We have explored the dangers of "Road Rage" and the reality of the "Collision," but the benefit of this journey is the restoration found in the "Body Shop." To stay on the right path, commit to a daily check of your "GPS" — the Word of God — and keep your "Passengers" (your family) at the center of your mission. By following the Map instead of your ego, you ensure that your journey doesn't just end but arrives at the Eternal City.

Bibliography

Holy Bible, New International Version, NIV®. Grand Rapids, MI: Zondervan, 2011. (Original work published 1973.)

Holy Bible, New King James Version, NKJV®. Nashville: Thomas Nelson, 1982.

Augustine of Hippo. *Confessions*. Translated by Henry Chadwick. Oxford: Oxford University Press, 1991.

Bainton, Roland H. *Here I Stand: A Life of Martin Luther*. New York: Abingdon Cokesbury Press, 1950.

Bonhoeffer, Dietrich. *Life Together*. Translated by John W. Doberstein. New York: HarperOne, 1954.

Cash, Johnny, and Patrick Carr. *Cash: The Autobiography*. New York: HarperCollins, 1997.

Colson, Charles. *Born Again*. Old Tappan: Chosen Books, 1976.

Elliot, Elisabeth. *Through Gates of Splendor*. Wheaton: Tyndale House, 1956.

Elliot, Jim. *The Journals of Jim Elliot*. Edited by Elisabeth Elliot. Old Tappan: Fleming H. Revell, 1978.

Frodsham, Stanley Howard. *Smith Wigglesworth: Apostle of Faith*. Springfield: Gospel Publishing House, 1948.

Graham, Billy. *Just As I Am: The Autobiography of Billy Graham*. New York: HarperCollins, 1997.

Hack, Richard. *Hughes: The Private Diaries, Memos and Letters*. Beverly Hills: New Millennium Press, 2001.

Hillis, Dick. *China Assignment*. San Jose: Overseas Crusades, 1967.

Magnusson, Sally. *The Flying Scotsman: A Biography*. New York: Quartet Books, 1981.

Mandela, Nelson. *Long Walk to Freedom*. Boston: Little, Brown and Company, 1994.

Metaxas, Eric. *Amazing Grace: William Wilberforce and the Heroic Campaign to End Slavery*. New York: HarperOne, 2007.

Metaxas, Eric. *Bonhoeffer: Pastor, Martyr, Prophet, Spy*. Nashville: Thomas Nelson, 2010.

Müller, George. *The Autobiography of George Müller*. New Kensington: Whitaker House, 1984.

Newton, John. *Out of the Depths: The Autobiography of John Newton*. Grand Rapids: Kregel, 2003.

Snyder, James. *In Pursuit of God: The Life of A.W. Tozer*. Camp Hill: Christian Publications, 1991.

Steer, Roger. *George Müller: Delighted in God*. Wheaton: Harold Shaw Publishers, 1997.

ten Boom, Corrie, John Sherrill, and Elizabeth Sherrill. *The Hiding Place*. Old Tappan: Chosen Books, 1971.

Tozer, A. W. *The Pursuit of God*. Camp Hill: Christian Publications, 1982.

Turner, Steve. *Amazing Grace: John Newton, Slavery, and the World's Most Enduring Song*. New York: HarperOne, 2002.

Turner, Steve. *The Man Called Cash: The Life, Love, and Faith of an American Legend*. Nashville: W Publishing Group, 2004.

Zamperini, Louis, and David Rensin. *Devil at My Heels*. New York: HarperCollins, 2003.

The Driver's Road

My Testimony

By Josmar Pereira

The Road I Started On

I was born the fifth of six children in the city of Ponta Grossa, in the state of Parana, Brazil. The road I was born on was already crowded with confusion. My mother was Catholic, with a mixture of Allan Kardec spiritism, Candomblé, and Macumba woven into the fabric of our home. My father carried his own collection of beliefs, a Buddha on his office shelf, a little spiritism, a little Protestantism, and a great deal of alcohol and pot and some other drugs. Every night he came home drunk, the house became a battlefield. Every morning the wreckage had to be survived before it could be cleaned up.

I loved Janete and I wanted to build something with her — a life that looked nothing like the one I had grown up in. We married in a Catholic ceremony in 1987, when I was seventeen years and ten months old. We were young, but we were determined. Together we made a decision that changed the course of our lives: we would leave Brazil, leave the violence and the poverty, and start fresh in the United States. At twenty-three, Janete and I arrived in Lynn, Massachusetts with our four-year-old daughter Ana. In 1997, our second daughter Victoria was born. We were building something. We just did not know what we were building it on. The Scriptures already had a word for what I was doing:

> *"There is a way that seems right to a man, but its end is the way of death." Proverbs 14:12 (NKJV)*

The Hollow Driver

For years I was what I would call a hollow Catholic. I went to mass when my agenda permitted. I believed in God the way a man believes in traffic laws, theoretically, from a distance, and mostly when it was convenient. The Bible was not a book I was allowed to open. I had been told since childhood that ordinary people who read it risked losing their minds. It was to be handled by priests, not by men like me.

So, I drove on my own navigation. Everything I built, I built with my own hands. Every deal I closed, I closed with my own strength. Every mile I covered, I covered on my own fuel. I was the king of my own road.

And then the road ended.

> *"Pride goes before destruction, and a haughty spirit before a fall."*
> *— Proverbs 16:18 (NKJV)*

The Driveway

I will not give you the clinical details of what happened on that day in November 2005. What I will tell you is this: I was sitting in my car, parked outside my own house, and the weight of everything I had built and lost was crushing me. The business was failing. The bank was threatening to take the house. A man I owed money to had called that day with threats that made the weight heavier still. And in that silence, a voice whispered to me that the people I loved would be better off without me on the road.

That was the enemy.

That same day, Ana came home from school early. God's providence was already at work, moving people into position before the storm broke completely. I ended up in the hospital that day and then was transferred to a mental health facility for two days. They released me the day before my birthday.

But here is what was happening while I was in those places, this is the part of the story that still brings me to tears.

Janete was desperate. She went to the Catholic church where we used to take the children, looking for help with the mortgage. She asked the priest if he could help. He told her to go to the back of the building. He walked her through one door, then another, into a small sanctuary. He pointed to a statue of Jesus and told her that was the only one who could help her. He told her to pray the rosary. And he sent her away.

She left that place with nothing. But something happened in that walk out the door, she realized that what she had just been offered was empty. A statue could not save her husband. A rosary could not stop the bank from taking her house. Religion had failed her at the moment she needed it most.

She went home. And there, in our living room, she got on her knees and grabbed our daughters Ana and Victoria, and for the first time she prayed to the real God. Not through a priest. Not to a statue. Not with a formula. Just a desperate woman opening her mouth and talking to a Father she was just beginning to know, asking Him to save her husband and her family.

He heard every word.

> *"The effective, fervent prayer of a righteous man avails much." — James 5:16 (NKJV)*

The Rescue

A former employee came to our house with a pastor. They prayed with me. They cried with me. And in the hospital, in the days that followed, I saw a Bible lying on a table. My spirit was thirsty in a way I had never felt before. I opened it — and even though the darkness in me fought what I was reading, something was cracking open.

They released me from the hospital the day before my birthday. And on a Sunday after Thanksgiving, an evangelical friend of Janete came to our house and invited us to church. I struggled to go. The enemy was still at the door. But we went.

What happened in that Brazilian church in East Boston on November 25, 2005 is something I will never be able to fully describe. I found myself on my knees, crying out loud, my clothes soaked as if I had been thrown into deep water. The weight was lifting. The chains were breaking. God was doing exactly what He had promised.

I was set free that night. Not by religion. Not by ritual. Not by a priest behind a curtain. By the living God who had been waiting for me to stop driving long enough for Him to reach me.

> *"Therefore if the Son makes you free, you shall be free indeed." — John 8:36 (NKJV)*

The Miracles Begin

The road after rescue was not immediately smooth. The house was still in danger. The money was still gone. But God was already moving.

That Thanksgiving week, just days after my salvation, there was a knock at our door. Our neighbors Christine and Susan had come together, one from the house on the right, one from across the street. They brought gift cards for the supermarket, a turkey, and early Christmas gifts for our daughters. Janete and I could not contain our tears.
We had told no one about our situation. God had told them.

Then at a Saturday night church service, people who barely knew us gathered around Janete and invited her into a consorcio, a group savings arrangement where members pool money and each takes a turn receiving the full amount. They had unanimously agreed that Janete would be the first to receive it. Strangers, moved by God, saving our house.

On January 15, 2006, God opened the door to steady employment at Cummings Properties in Woburn, Massachusetts. The road was beginning to stabilize. But the enemy was watching, and the moment I let my guard down, he moved.

> *"And my God shall supply all your need according to His riches in glory by Christ Jesus." — Philippians 4:19 (NKJV)*

The IRS and the Highway

Old debts have a way of finding you. Tax mistakes from the years when I was driving by my own navigation caught up with us. An IRS agent showed up at our door while I was at work, shaking her badge in Janete face, demanding payment and paperwork. When I came home that afternoon, the atmosphere in the house had changed completely. The fear was back. The accusations were back. The enemy was using old ammunition.

A wise colleague pointed me to an accountant who could help. On the day Janete and I drove to meet him; something broke on I-95 South. The pressure of everything, the debt, the fear, the accumulated weight of the years exploded between us. It was one of the most frightening moments of our marriage. I pulled to the breakdown lane. I stopped the car. With no vehicles behind us, I grabbed the wheel and prayed out loud right there on the highway. God again. Always God.

The accountant set up a payment plan. But we made it through. We always made it through, not because of our strength, but because of His.

> *"I can do all things through Christ who strengthens me." — Philippians 4:13 (NKJV)*

The Rooftop

Something remarkable happened during this season that I have never forgotten. I was on the rooftop of a building, helping with repairs, when my mind drifted to the story of Abraham bargaining with God over the destruction of Sodom. And suddenly, in the middle of my workday, I spoke to God about something that had been stirring in me a vision of people from every nation coming into the streets together to pray.

And God spoke back. Not in an audible voice the way we imagine it in movies. But clearly. Unmistakably. The Holy Spirit said to me: Can you do it?

I was standing on a rooftop in Massachusetts, a former hollow Catholic who had been saved less than a year, and God was giving me a vision. I went home and shared it with my family and friends. Nobody wanted to help. So, I did what Abraham did, I went back to God and started bargaining. Why me? It is too hard. Are You sure it was You who said that?

God is patient with the bargaining. He was patient with Abraham. He was patient with Moses. He was patient with me.

> *"For God has not given us a spirit of fear, but of power and of love and of a sound mind." 2 Timothy 1:7 (NKJV)*

The Angel at the Recruiting Station

In July 2006 there was a major accident on I-95 North. Traffic was completely stopped. I made a decision to take I-93 South toward Boston and cut through Malden to avoid it. And then, clearly and unmistakably, the Holy Spirit spoke to me: Pull into that parking lot. I obeyed. I parked. And the Spirit said: Go inside the Army Recruiting Station.

I had never been inside one of those buildings in my life. But I had already learned what happens when you grieve the Spirit, when you hear and do not move. So, I walked toward the door. There was a soldier standing outside, smoking. He looked at me and said: Ask for the Chaplain Assistant position.

I went inside, a recruiter came and greeted me, he asked what I was looking for, if I want to join in. How could I have told this man that I just come in because I heard the Holy Spirit speaking to me in the car and told me to stop there? I said, I don't know, he looked puzzled. I mentioned the soldier at the door, the one who told me to ask for the Chaplain Assistant position. The sergeant looked at me and said: I have been the only one here all week. There was nobody outside that door. He then asked my age. I said thirty-seven. He told me the cutoff age was thirty-four. He said leave your number and maybe things will change, I left. But several weeks later, Janete told me someone from the Army had called and left a message.

I called back. They told me that the cut-off age was changed to forty-two. God had already moved the boundary.

On January 6, 2007, I left Massachusetts for basic training at Fort Knox, Kentucky. Blind faith. Total obedience. And God had already arranged everything my family would need while I was gone.

> *"Do not forget to entertain strangers, for by so doing some have unwittingly entertained angels." — Hebrews 13:2 (NKJV)*

The Road Through Iraq

Military service took me to Iraq not as chaplain assistant, but as truck driver. The details of what happened there are written on my body and in my memory in ways that words struggle to reach. What I can tell you is that on a day when the motor pool was in chaos over a damaged tire, I was working underneath a vehicle. When I crawled out, I struck my head on a light casing. A fellow soldier caught me before I hit the ground.

I am a man. I told myself I was fine. I kept working. It was not until my battle buddy and I saw the cut in my head under the cap at chow, when I had to wet my cap to remove it, that anyone knew how serious it was. Hours later, my body began to shake. My platoon sergeant took one look at me and sent me to the field hospital immediately.

I woke up on a plane, not knowing where I was going. The attendant looked at me and said: Glad you are awake. We almost lost you.

The road through recovery from a Traumatic Brain Injury is long and difficult and often invisible to everyone around you. The system that was supposed to have my back disappeared. But God did not disappear.

I want to say something to every man who has served and come back carrying something invisible: God sees what the system misses. He does not forget the miles you drove in service to others. He is the Master Mechanic, and no damage is beyond His ability to restore.

> *"Yea, though I walk through the valley of the shadow of death, I will fear no evil; for You are with me." — Psalm 23:4 (NKJV)*

The Cancer

In 2012, one year after my medical retirement from the Army, Janete was diagnosed with breast cancer.

I want you to sit with that for a moment. The woman who had been on her knees in the living room praying for me while I sat in that driveway. The woman who had cleaned houses to keep us afloat. The woman who had stood beside me through every mile of the hardest road. She now has cancer.

But God had already moved. Because of my military service, we had real insurance coverage for the first time in our lives. The treatment cost us nothing. The care was immediate and thorough. And our daughter Ana, who had been born with a bicuspid heart valve and had been essentially ignored by doctors for years because we had no adequate coverage, was able to get the heart ablation surgery she needed. She had come home from school early on the day my road collapsed. God had been watching over her since that day.

God had sent me into the Army not just for my calling. He had sent me in to cover my family. He knew what was coming. He always knows what is coming.

> *"For I know the thoughts that I think toward you, says the Lord, thoughts of peace and not of evil, to give you a future and a hope." — Jeremiah 29:11 (NKJV)*

The Father

In July 2010, my sister called from Brazil. My father, the man whose drunken rages had sent me running at seventeen, the man with the Buddha on his shelf and the bottle in his hand was dying. Cancer had returned after years of remission.

My finances were not stable enough for an international trip. I spent an entire day applying for every emergency assistance program available through the Army. Every answer was no. As I drove home that evening, exhausted, approaching exit 40 on I-95 North, I prayed out loud: God, this is all in Your hands. If it is for me to go, make it available.

The phone rang before I reached the exit. A woman told me they would pay for my plane ticket. I don't know who she was, I'll never know, but God knows.

Thanks to the angel that God sent to bless me, I arrived in Brazil. My brother in-law was excited, he couldn't believe that I was there, I didn't know the surprise God had prepared for me, on the Sunday after my arrival, I stood beside my father with my young sister Lu and my brother Jackson as he was baptized in the name of Jesus Christ. The man I had remembered as an alcoholic who beat my siblings and my mother when drunk. The man who had also taken me to the movie theater on good days. That man, my father, professed Jesus Christ as Lord and Savior.

The Holy Spirit used me to help him call each of his children by name, asking for forgiveness and speaking blessing over each one for the last time. I helped the man who had wounded me bless the people he had wounded. That is what God does with restored drivers. He sends them back to repair the roads they damaged.

> *"And we know that all things work together for good to those who love God, to those who are called according to His purpose." — Romans 8:28 (NKJV)*

What the Road Has Taught Me

I graduated from two colleges by the grace of God. I tell you that plainly because I want you to understand what grace means in practical terms. After a traumatic brain injury, maintaining academic focus is not a small thing. But God does not call the equipped — He equips the called.

There are more miracles than I can fit on these pages. More moments where God showed up when the road was closed and the fuel was gone and the engine was smoking. I could write another book, and perhaps I will. John said it best:

> *"And there are also many other things that Jesus did, which if they were written one by one, I suppose that even the world itself could not contain the books that would be written." — John 21:25 (NKJV)*

The Invitation

I wrote this book because I know what it is to drive the wrong road at full speed. I know what it is to hit the wall. I know what it is to sit in a driveway with the weight of a collapsed world on your chest and hear a voice telling you the road is over.

And I know, I know with every mile of my road that the voice was lying.

The road is not over. The Master Mechanic is still working. The GPS is still speaking. The Eternal City is still the destination.

You are not too far gone. You have not driven too far in the wrong direction. You have not made too many wrong turns. I am living proof that God will find you in your driveway, in your hospital room, on your rooftop, on a traffic detour on I-95, on a plane you woke up on not knowing where you were going.

He found me in all of those places. He will find you too.

Open your mouth. Talk to Him. He is already listening.

"Call to Me, and I will answer you, and show you great and mighty things, which you do not know." — Jeremiah 33:3 (NKJV)

Drive on, brother. The Eternal City is worth every mile.

Josmar Pereira
Sanford, Maine, 2026

Acknowledgments

I would like to thank my wife, Janete, for her unwavering support during the miles we travelled together. I am also grateful to my family for their patience and for being the "passengers" that make this drive worthwhile. Most importantly, I thank the God the Master Mechanic for picking up the pieces of my life and showing me the Way of the Cross when I was lost.

About the Author

Josmar Pereira is a veteran of the United States Army (2007–2011) and a dedicated business owner, and a credentialed minister with the Assemblies of God in Northen New England Ministry Network. He holds a Master's degree completed in 2025, and is actively pursuing a Doctor Degree in Urban Ministry, he combines disciplined leadership with a deep passion for spiritual growth. A trilingual communicator fluent in English, Portuguese, and Spanish, Josmar brings a global perspective to his writing. He resides in Sanford, Maine, with his wife, Janete, and finds his greatest joy in traveling with his daughters and granddaughter. The Highway of Life is his first devotional aimed at helping men navigate their spiritual journey with precision and purpose.